Embroidery from
Traditional English Patterns

Embroidery from Traditional English Patterns

Ruby Evans

B T Batsford Limited   London
Charles T Branford Company
Newton Centre   Massachusetts

First published 1971
7134 2649 7
Library of Congress Catalog Card Number 75-131433
Branford SBN 8231 4026 1

Filmset by Keyspools Ltd Golborne Lancs
Printed in Great Britain by
Taylor, Garnett Evans & Co Ltd
for the publishers
B T Batsford Limited
4 Fitzhardinge Street London W1 and
Charles T Branford Company
28 Union Street Newton Centre Massachusetts 02159

Contents

Acknowledgment

The author would like to acknowledge with gratitude the assistance of Mr Ronald G Brewster, ARPS, who took all the photographs; Mrs Win Taylor who made the tablecloth shown on page 67, and Mrs Irene Dixon who made the apron shown on page 67 and the summer skirt shown on page 79.

Thanks are also extended to museum curators and owners of smocks from whom some of the pattern details were obtained, and to many students whose experiments went into the making of this book.

All other needlework illustrated in the book was carried out by the author.

Introduction

This book presents new ideas from an old source. It is planned to give pleasure and practical help to the beginner who makes useful articles for her family as well as the advanced worker who regards embroidery as an art form.

My own experience of guiding and talking to countless needlewomen convinces me that there is a wealth of natural talent and unexplored skill not often realised. A little help in starting, overcoming first problems or considering an ambitious project, can result in work which is both enjoyable and satisfying. Few exact rules, measurements or procedures are given, only suggestions and ideas personally tried out. It is hoped that those who enjoy sewing may find here some new ideas, quicker processes or fresh themes.

The designs in this book have been inspired by the borders and motifs embroidered in the past by mothers, wives and sweethearts on their menfolk's smocks. Some of these simple, imaginative patterns have already been discovered and used by present day embroidery groups seeking new ideas. While the selection in this book is by no means exhaustive, it contains many designs brought to light by happy hunting in museums and private collections all over the country. My students and I have experimented with the patterns, retaining their character while adapting them to practical contemporary taste. The original work was, of necessity, done with coarse unbleached threads on heavy homespun linen. When combined with our wider range of colours, threads and fabrics, the old designs provide a rewarding field for the needlewoman today.

The stitches are few and simple. The basic feather stitch, quick to learn and to work, is known to most women from personal use or childhood. Blanket stitch and chainstitch, equally well known, are the only other stitches usually needed. In the full size charts given here, some borders are in their original form. Others have been simplified to remove confusing detail or to suit modern taste, for though a richly worked pattern is attractive, less elaborate but equally pleasing effects can be achieved in a shorter time. Variety of colour has been introduced, and some braids, especially the narrow wavy ric-rac, have been used to replace tedious lines of stitching.

It has been said that the details on the smocks bore some relation to the trade of the wearer: crooks and sheep-pens for the shepherd, flowers for the gardener, winding lanes for the waggoner, hops for the drayman, hearts for the milkmaid. It is a pleasant thought that a farmer at a hiring fair might have known a man's trade from his smock. However, it is more likely that the resourceful rural needle-woman was inspired by ordinary countryside objects, the murals on the church walls or perhaps by freehand doodling such as we find on old clay pots and everyday items. It is even more probable that the patterns were of family or local tradition.

There is a strong regional likeness in the patterns, as might be expected when few villagers went far from home. Thus there are triple curves, possibly inspired by a winding stream, on the smocks from Surrey, Sussex and Kent; the angular borders of Essex, East Anglia and the East Midlands; the chain stitch spirals of Wales; the elaborate close stitched patterns of Warwick, Worcester and Shropshire; the floral designs of Hampshire and the West Country.

Some designs turn up all over the country, notably those which include the heart, varying in size and shape from county to county. No doubt there was a sacred significance in its use, and it was probably thought of as an amulet or good luck motif or perhaps a sign of true love.

Whatever the long-lost reasons for the original details, the practice of identifying the various designs as *Shepherd, Gardener* or *Waggoner* is a convenient one and has been used throughout this book. There is no doubt that with a little imagination almost any trade can be read into any design!

All the designs given here can be used in many ways to suit many tastes and needs. Copy them or adapt them, make them simpler or more elaborate, work them on useful articles or consider them as purely decorative patterns. But, above all, enjoy them.

Part 1

1 Materials and threads

Choice of material should be dictated by personal taste and the purpose of the finished article. Linen is still a favourite for table items, where washing and wearing factors are important, but many other modern fabrics are equally good. Firm cottons are ideal for many purposes and come in a wealth of different types, from soft dress-weights for aprons and children's garments to denim and sailcloth for cushions and panels.

Materials with a drip-dry finish are best avoided, as they are difficult to stitch and are inclined to pucker. Entirely man-made fabrics can also be difficult, as they tend to fray easily and to pull out of shape. However, mixtures of man-made and natural fibres, such as certain furnishing fabrics, are pleasant to use and give excellent results. They are available in a wide range of attractive, vibrant colours and various surface ribs and weaves. A plain, rather than a patterned background, is usually a good choice, but stripes (see photograph *6b*) or a light pattern can sometimes be used to advantage. Just looking at a piece of material will often inspire the embroiderer to use it in a particular way.

For bold effects light-weight embroidery felt is ideal. A splendid range of colours is produced. It is pleasant to handle, does not fray, and suits contemporary taste.

Some materials which seem unsuitable because they are too soft, stretchy or frayable can be successfully used if backed with a bonded, non-woven interlining such as *vilene* and embroidered through both layers. This type of interlining is used widely for dressmaking, but embroiderers also find it useful as it resists creasing, does not fray and can be washed or dry-cleaned without shrinking or stretching. It can be purchased inexpensively in dress fabric departments or shops. Suggestions for its use are given in chapter 4 and in the later detailed chapters.

Most linen and cotton fabrics will shrink to some extent when washed, so it is a good idea to shrink them first. To do this without creasing or losing the crisp new look, wring out a large tea towel or piece of sheeting in water, leaving it quite damp. Spread it out flat and lay the fabric smoothly upon it. Fold the whole thing neatly together, put in a polythene bag and leave for twelve hours, but **not longer.** Take out the fabric and press with a fairly hot iron until perfectly dry.

If using non-woven interlining, it will not shrink, so deal with the fabric before applying it. Man-made fabrics do not usually need shrinking unless they contain a large proportion of cotton.

A word of warning is needed about using felt. As this is bonded, not woven, **never** damp it at any stage of the work, or it will lose its shape. Press it with a dry iron which is not too hot. Iron-on interlining is excellent for keeping felt in shape while working, and the finished article can be pressed without damping to remove working creases.

The material described here is intended only as a guide. Many other materials could be equally well chosen to suit the worker's taste, purpose or shopping facilities.

Embroidery threads

Most threads give good results, and there is no need to keep to one kind only. Different thicknesses, some bright and some dull, can blend most effectively in one piece of work.

The round, softly twisted threads, such as *pearl cotton* or *sylko perlé* (known to many by the old name of *star sylko*) are easy to use. They are mercerised, which gives them a pleasing sheen, and usually come in small balls, No 8 fine and No 5 a little thicker.

If a matt finish is preferred, coton-à-broder or stranded cotton are more suitable. Coton-à-broder is a fine, soft, round thread. Most stores stock it in black and white in small skeins, and large or specialist stores stock it in a wide range of colours. Stranded cotton is readily available in many colours and has the advantage of being easily divided into whatever thickness is required. The full six strands are usually too much, giving a clumsy finish. Four strands are better; three for small, neat stitching or a good deal of close work.

These are the best known threads, but some embroiderers have other favourites or find different ones locally. There are thicker soft threads for those who like large, bold stitching, or finer ones can be used double, but on the whole finer threads give better definition. Some man-made threads, especially rayon, are becoming popular and give a pleasant silky finish. They are a little more difficult to use, as they need a twist of the needle at intervals to prevent knotting or unravelling, but this soon becomes routine.

Narrow braid, couched down with embroidery thread, offers a quick, attractive way to deal with long straight lines where an extensive border is planned, perhaps on an apron or skirt, or round the edges of mats or tablecloths. The very fine, wavy ric-rac is ideal and can be used in different ways. The stores trimming department may yield other suitable styles, including straight-edged ridged braid. Most are inexpensive and come in black, white and bright colours which are usually fast, but it is wise to wash them first for use on very pale backgrounds. (Suggestions for braid on pages 25 and 26.)

2 Choosing colours

Using colour in any craft needs thought and consideration. Some people have a natural sense of harmony and contrast, or have learned from experience, or have a personal preference for certain shades. They may not need the suggestions given in this chapter.

Others may be unsure of themselves, and may waste excellent work on a poor colour choice. It sometimes happens that extremely competent needlewoman, able to do splendid work, will limit their efforts to pastel pinks and blues on a cream ground, or match up the exact colours in carpets or curtains – both safe, but rather dull and a little out-of-date.

Although the more traditional needlewoman still uses white or cream backgrounds and pastel threads, there is a movement today towards deep or vivid backgrounds, highlighted with strong contrasts, suiting the vibrant colours of contemporary furnishing.

The borders and motifs in this book lend themselves particularly well to such colour schemes. Deep blue, dark maroon or bottle green are good backgrounds for stitchery in pale colours. Grounds of bright gold, turquoise blue, shocking pink or grass green will take embroidery in black. Pale, clear shades, such as silver grey or primrose, will set off stitchery in vivid colours.

Some colour detail is given with each of the items illustrated. Whether these or other colours are chosen, the tone values may be found useful.

The following suggestions may help the beginner or give new ideas to the experienced worker.

1   Two shades of one colour with a splash of a strong contrast make a good scheme; for instance, soft lilac and deep purple with a very little hot pink, or two muted greens with brilliant gold. Black and white with a touch of any vivid shade is also very effective. But avoid *equal* amounts of the two main colours, or they will fight for attention and lead to a confused result. Use rather more of one than the other, with a very little of the third.

2   One colour only, especially black or white, can be striking on a strongly contrasting background. Examples are the wall panel in colour plate 2 with black stitchery on a brilliant ground of flame, pink and lime. The deep pink and natural cushion in colour plate 3 again has an all black design; and the deep blue cushion in photograph 12a has white embroidery only. If dead white or black are

16

Place mats: designs from
a   Miller   chart 4
b   Wheelwright   chart 5
c   Gardener   chart 8

Plate 1

thought to be too severe, try a similar one colour effect with off-white or oyster, or what might be called off-black, such as navy blue, bitter-chocolate, or deep ivy green. For still more striking effects within the one colour scheme, use threads of different thicknesses, or one glossy and one matt.

3   A wider range of colours can look attractive if well thought out, but too many unrelated shades look gaudy and confused, unless a sombre shade is added to tone down the bright ones.

4   A better idea to add life and movement to a piece of work is to use two very similar shades placed close together. For instance, blanket stitch could be worked in light red and whipped with scarlet, or feather stitch worked with forget-me-not blue and whipped with royal. Take care, however, that the two threads are very close in colour, especially when whipping chain stitch. Otherwise, as mentioned in (1) above, the two separate colours may give an unsatisfactory result. Using whipped stitches can be a useful colour device. (Chapter 3, page *20* and diagram *1e, f, g* and *h*.)

5   When a border is to go downwards, as on the wall panel or magazine cover (colour plate *2*), or workbag (colour plate *4*), the colours used on each side should balance, though not necessarily be the same. But if a border goes across, as on a skirt, apron, tea cosy or chairback, it sometimes improves the effect if there is a slight weight of colour in the lower part. A similar treatment could be used on a circular design, as shown on the round tablecloth (photograph *8*), where the outer scalloped border is in black, and the twisted border just within it is a deeper blue than the similar border on the inside of the design.

6   Choosing one's own colour scheme, rather than following instructions, gives a fresh and individual result, but is often found difficult. A great deal can be learned by looking more consciously at one's own surroundings. Note the blending of shades on a flower-bed, a butterfly on a leaf, the changing colours of water in a lake, or leaf sprays and trees at different times of year. Observe the colour in magazines, shop window displays or rows of books on the library shelves.

3 Stitches

The three popular traditional stitches, blanket, feather and chain, are equally effective today. They can be worked in their simplest form, or varied to give a more contemporary effect or a more subtle use of colour. A few other well known stitches have been sparingly used in the articles illustrated. More elaborate stitches may be employed to suit personal taste, but the designs are better suited to simple methods.

Details of working can be followed from the diagrams and photographs (diagrams 1, 2 and 3, photographs 1 and 2), and the overall effect can be observed in later photographs. For ease of working, first ensure that needle and thread are right for each other. Crewel needles with long eyes suit most embroidery threads. Try out different sizes with the thread and fabric to be used, matching needle, thread and fabric for comfortable handling.

Blanket stitch   diagram 1a, photograph 1a

With some variation of closeness and direction, this is also known as buttonhole or single feather. It is a simple looped stitch. The spines can stand out as right angles or lie at a slope, and the stitch can be worked in either direction.

Feather stitch   diagram 1b, photograph 1a

Possibly one of the oldest and most versatile of embroidery stitches. It is individual to each embroiderer, rather like one's handwriting or knitting tension. Use a long thread in the needle, for the work grows quickly. Basically, the stitch is similar to blanket stitch, the loops being worked alternately to right and left, but it is usually worked downwards. The stitch takes on a different appearance according to the angle of the needle, the amount of fabric picked up and the space between the stitches. The best effect comes from close, small stitches.

Chain stitch   diagram 1c, photograph 1a

A closed loop stitch with many variations. Some are shown in diagram 1d, g and h, and photographs 1b and 2c, and are described later in this chapter.

18

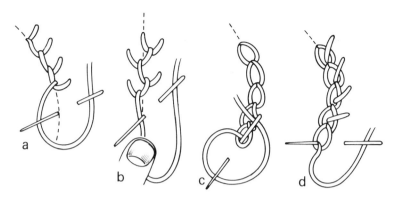

Diagram 1   Basic stitches

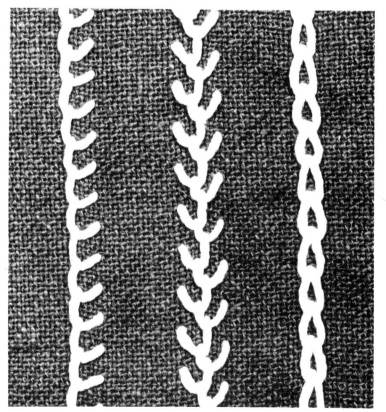

Photograph 1a   Three basic stitches: blanket, feather and chain

Whipped edges   diagrams *1e, f, g* and *h*, photographs *1b* and *2c*

By whipping the main edges of blanket, feather or chain stitch, the edge often becomes bolder and more distinctive. Colour effects can also be intensified (see page *17*). The basic method is to work the original stitch with a fairly loose tension; then with a needle and separate thread, to pick up each stitch of the main line. Compare diagrams *1e, 1f* and *1g* where the method is expanded, with photographs *1b* and *2c* which show the finished appearance. The whipping thread is fastened to the back of the work at the beginning, brought to the front, and does not enter the fabric again until it is finished off on the wrong side at the end of the line. Stitches can be whipped left to right or right to left. Care must be taken not to pick up any of the fabric on the point of the needle. To avoid this, some workers put the eye, rather than the point, through each stitch (diagram *1h*) but this can result in a pricked finger! Actually, whipping is very easy and pleasant to do. Keep the tension fairly loose, as it tends to draw the line up a little.

Not every type of stitch needs whipping, and some edges look better and bolder without it. Feather stitch often looks better as it is, but blanket stitch takes on a more regular, raised edge when whipped, and chain stitch lends itself particularly well to variations of whipping (photograph *2c*).

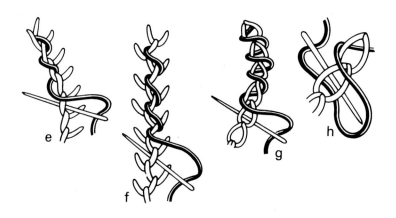

Diagram 1   Basic stitches   *continued*

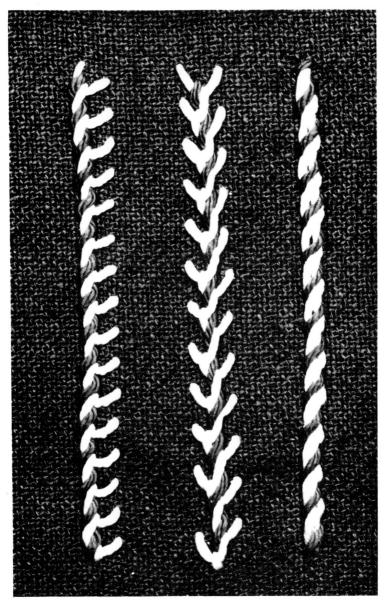

Photograph 1b   Whipping the three basic stitches

When these three stitches have been tried out in their basic form, the worker may like to experiment with other ways of using them. Photograph 2 shows variations which have been used in the articles illustrated. Photograph 2a shows blanket stitch worked with alternately long and short spines and two lines facing in towards each other. This stitch could also be worked in two lines back to back with the spines facing outwards, and the main lines could be whipped together.

Photograph 2b shows zigzag feather stitch, a great favourite and suitable to many of the designs. Instead of one stitch right and left alternately, two stitches are made on each side. To make a wider zigzag, three or more stitches can be made on each side alternately. Note from these two variations the difference made by placing the needle at a different angle. The first is sometimes known as closed feather stitch, and the needle enters the fabric almost straight down-

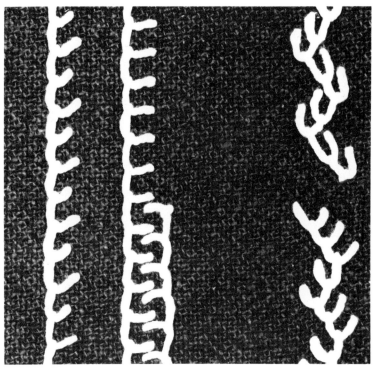

Photograph 2a   Variations of blanket stitch   2b   Variations of feather

wards. The second is a more open stitch, with the needle placed diagonally (diagram 1b).

Chain stitch offers the most scope for effective variations in whipping. When whipped, as in diagram 1g, the result is a raised cord, as shown in photograph 1b. When a feathered chain (diagram 1d) has been worked, the 'feathers' are left free, and only the main chain whipped. Photograph 2c shows two types of whipped and feather chain, and also two other variations of whipping as follows. If each side of the chain is whipped separately, but in alternate directions, the result is a fine plait (variation 3). If two rows of chain stitch are worked quite closely side by side, and their adjacent edges whipped together, a broad decorative line is obtained.

Whipping need not be done in the same type of thread as the basic stitch. A stranded cotton, using three threads, whips well on a round twisted thread, or try a finer thread on a thicker basic.

Photograph 2c   Four variations of whipping chain stitch

Stem stitch   diagram *2d*

This gives a clear, fine line. It is usually worked upwards, and the stitches will be longer or shorter according to the angle of the needle. Long stitches give a finer line, shorter stitches a more compact but wider line, depending also on the thickness of the thread.

Satin stitch   diagram *2c*

Useful for giving a solid centre to small shapes, thus contrasting with more open, flowing lines. The needle is placed at an angle so that the stitches are straight and lie close together. A soft, easily spreading thread gives the best results, as there should be no fabric showing between the stitches. Care must be taken to keep a neat edge.

Detached chain stitch   diagram *2b*

A chain worked singly rather than in a continuous line. Also known as lazy-daisy, it became unpopular because it was so often carelessly worked in long loose stitches to make daisy-type flowers with little character. However, in the right setting, as within flowers in the gardener design, it can be most effective (see *sun dress* photograph *13a* and page 78).

Fly stitch   diagram *2a*

A variation of chain stitch, with separate stitches open instead of closed at the top. It can be worked either downwards or in horizontal lines. The fly stitch is shown as a method of couching ridged braid (downwards) and decorating ric-rac (horizontal) in diagram *3*.

Hem stitch   diagram *2e*

Originally an elaborate form of needlework which involved drawing threads from the material and grouping them in many ways with tied stitches. In its simplest form, the handkerchief hem makes a good finish on linen or similar fabric, especially where the hem is required to lie flat, as on a table mat or chairback. The threads are drawn first and a hem turned and tacked. In regular sequence, the threads are picked up in bundles to tie them, and each time a small stitch is worked above the bundle and into the hem. This stitch can look effective when the hem is turned on to the right side. If the withdrawn area is more than a few threads, a matching line of stitches should be worked along the lower edge, so that the tied threads lie in straight bars.

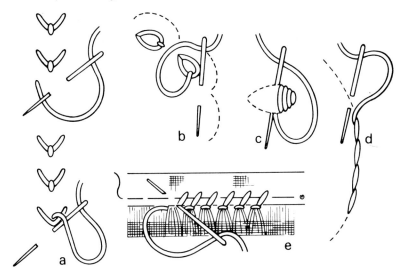

Diagram 2   Other useful stitches

Using braid   diagram 3

As already mentioned, various types of fine braid can save time and give a striking finish to a long border (photograph 5) or divide the sections of a large design (colour plate 3). Securing it to the material is an easy matter, but for good results the braid should be narrow and sewn down *exactly* on the line. To ensure this, avoid trusting the eye; tack the braid in place before stitching it down. Diagram 3 shows ways to secure the braid. Diagram 3a and the apron in photograph 5 show a very narrow, straight braid with a central rib, sewn down with fly stitches. Diagram 3b, c and d show ways to use ric-rac braid. The method of securing this will depend not only on personal taste but the amount of wear the finished article will get and the position of the braid. On a little decorative mat, catching the braid down with embroidery thread in diagonal stitches across the narrowest part may be quite sufficient (diagram

3b). On a cushion or apron which will have hard wear, tiny stitches along the crest of each wave would be better (diagram *3c*). Firmer methods may be required when the braid is used at the edge of an article or becomes part of a seam, as in the child's sectional cap, described on page *88* and seen in colour plate *2*. Diagram *3d* shows an added line of fly stitch which might be used in this case.

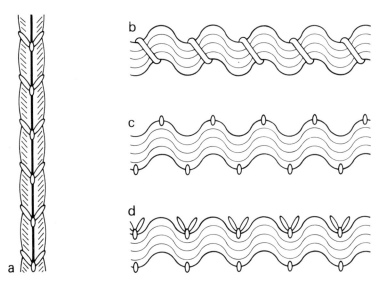

Diagram 3   Using braid

Beginning and ending

When working on a single thickness of material, the best way to begin is to run three or four tiny stitches upwards along the line to the starting point. If this is too bulky or otherwise inconvenient, leave a tail of thread on the wrong side, and when the stitching has been worked, thread up the tail and fasten off on the wrong side beneath the first stitches.

To finish off, take the thread through to the back of the work and run a few stitches into the back of the last stitches.

Where the material is backed with an interlining, it is a simple matter to begin and end with a few stitches into this at the back of the work. It is also possible and often very time-saving to 'travel' carefully from one part of the design to another by running tiny stitches through the interlining only, but take care not to pucker the work.

A final word of encouragement. Some needlewomen, even the most skilful ones, doubt their ability to keep freehand stitches even. Whilst it is obvious that personal ability and practice are important, there are a great many simple ways to provide a guide for size, width and spacing when working the various stitches. These are described in the next two chapters.

4   Making a start

Deal with the most important decisions first. What to make, material and threads are obviously the first considerations. Size, design and colour follow, depending one on the other. Details such as choice of stitches and methods of finishing must be thought out next if they affect the first preparation, but much can be decided as the work grows.

For enjoyment and a good result, consider the amount of work involved in a project. Unless sure of skill and the time available, avoid a large or complicated undertaking. The beginner might make a cushion, a tea cosy or a mat, and, discovering personal preferences, become an expert in due course, embarking on a wall panel, a wide skirt border or a large tablecloth. To begin the other way round might result in an unfinished masterpiece!

Planning size and shape

However simple the shape, it is a good idea to cut a paper pattern of the chosen article. Allow for turnings and tack them in place, so that the finished size can be seen and tried out. For instance, cut a paper placemat and try it on the table. See how a set of four mats would look and how they could be cut from available material. Often a small variation of width or length would suit the table better or fit without waste into material to be purchased.

Try a paper chairback on the chair, to see that it lies well over the top edge or against the curved sides. Compare a paper cushion, apron or workbag pattern against the measurements of those in use.

Choose a design to suit the size of the article, with the stitches which are liked best. The repeats of the pattern should be in proportion to the finished size. For instance, a small fold-over handbag calls for a neat border with a small repeat (photograph 7b), while a long coffee-table mat can take a larger one (photograph 12b). Plan the design on the paper pattern, measuring the length of the repeat on the chart, and estimating how many repeats can be used. Begin planning in the centre of the border, so that each end can terminate in the best place.

Aim always to work the whole of the stitchery on single fabric, ie before turning hems or making up waistbands or pockets. Not only does this make the stitching easier and more even, but it gives, on an apron or mat for instance, a chance to add or take away a little material to suit the ends of the repeat.

Cutting out

When size and other details are decided, press the material lightly to remove creases and give the smoothest possible surface. Cut out the various parts, either by laying the pattern in place or by taking

Photograph 3   Trial pieces

measurements from it. Before cutting out, check the grain of the material, and if possible draw a thread to ensure cutting all edges straight. These may seem obvious points, but they can make much difference to the ease and final success of the work.

Frayable edges need overcasting with large stitches (photograph 3), or quickly binding with narrow strips of thin waste material. Where *vilene* is used, the iron-on type should be pressed to the wrong side of the fabric at this stage. If using sew-on *vilene* it is usually better to apply the design to the material first, then tack the interlining to the wrong side. Tack across the work in several directions, then overcast the material down to the *vilene* as shown in photograph 3. This enables the edges to be freed when the embroidery is finished, and recut or arranged as required.

Whether to use sew-on or iron-on interlining is a matter of taste. A very light-weight sew-on grade is usually preferred for linen, cotton and similar frayable materials, and iron-on for felt. Always keep it as light in weight as possible, just sufficient to give the necessary backing, so that the material retains its character and texture.

At this stage, a trial piece of work on spare material can be helpful in assessing stitch and colour detail. Photograph 3 shows some ways to do this. It takes a little extra time which may be grudged in the enthusiasm of starting the main work, but it can prevent much unpicking or accepting stitches and colours finally disliked.

5 Transfers and tracings

Designs can be applied to material by means of an iron-on embroidery transfer, a tracing taken from the given charts or cut-out paper shapes. Choose the most suitable for taste, skill and circumstances.

Using an embroidery transfer

This is an easy and popular method. It tends to commit the worker to a set design, but has advantages for needlewomen who enjoy the pleasing rhythm of embroidery without the effort or equipment required for other methods.

When used intelligently, a transfer worked with enjoyment may well lead to enthusiasm for more advanced or creative projects. Although the design can be worked exactly as it is, there is plenty of scope for blocking out parts not required with gummed paper or cutting up and rearranging the transfer to fit a desired space.

Blue transfers are usually best for fabrics in light or bright colours, and are the most widely used. Yellow or silver are better for dark backgrounds and are also good when a light impression is needed on a delicate light colour. A mid-blue fabric does not accept any transfer colour well.

Before applying any transfer, press the material well, especially if the surface has any kind of raised weave, and decide exactly where to place the transfer. If a long length, mark the upper and lower boundary with lines of tacking. Lay the transfer carefully in place, pinning or tacking along the top edge. Cut away any reference number or other wording; this can be used to test the heat of the iron on a spare piece of material. Press every part of the transfer, and raise the paper to see that the impression is good. If any parts are not clear, they can often be pressed again, providing the paper is not moved.

Using tracing paper diagram 4

This method is an excellent way to make use of any outlined pattern from a magazine, book or other source, and is particularly suitable for the charts given here. It enables an embroiderer either to work the given design, or to select any part to suit her purpose. Special transparent tracing paper can be purchased from a stationer, but ordinary kitchen greaseproof paper is almost as good. Some

31

sheets of dressmakers' carbon paper will also be required. Dress-making accessory shops and some stationers sell this, usually in assorted packets of red, yellow and blue made by *Milwards* and others. It is much cleaner in use than typewriter carbon paper which should be avoided.

Cut a piece of tracing paper to the size needed, allowing a little extra width round the boundaries of the design. Lay it over the chart, and trace with a sharp pencil every line required to be used. Some like to move the paper along and trace off the whole of a long border. Others may prefer to trace two or three repeats of the design, with sufficient at each end to 'key' the design into place.

On the material, press a crease or mark with tacking the exact centre line and the boundaries of the design. It is also a good idea to mark with short tacking lines the boundary of each repeat, es-pecially if it is a long one such as the *Shepherd*. Thus a tracing can easily be repeated over and over again in the right place, though the tracing paper may wear and need renewing if it is a long border for an apron or skirt. Place the material on a hard, firm surface, pin or tack the tracing along the top edge, and slip the dressmakers' carbon between tracing and material as shown in diagram 4. Go over every line firmly with a tracing wheel or a point such as on a fine knitting needle, taking care that the tracing paper does not move. Lift a corner of the tracing from time to time, to make sure of using sufficient pressure for a clear impression.

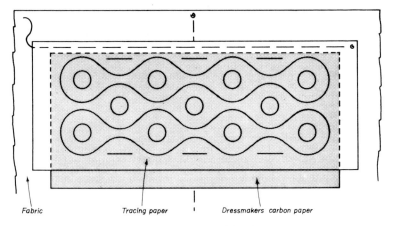

Diagram 4   Applying a design to material using tracing paper

Where dressmakers' carbon paper cannot be obtained, and all that is available is material, chart, pencil and kitchen paper, the following time-honoured method is useful. Make a tracing, lay it pencil-side downwards on the material. Go over every line with pencil, using a fair amount of pressure. This should give a clear outline on the material. Repeat this process along the border, each time reversing the tracing. With care and a very sharp pencil it gives good results, though the pencil marks can soil delicate work.

Whatever method is used, the impression may wear away slightly on a long piece of work. It is therefore better to trace a small area at a time. When, in spite of this, some lines fade, keep a ballpoint handy and strengthen the lines lightly as the stitching approaches them. If it is a good quality ballpoint this is cleaner and more satisfactory than using a pencil. The lines can be hidden, as most of the stitches are spreading ones, and if kept light they will cause no trouble when the article is washed.

When tracing the borders from the given charts, it may be found better to trace only the basic parts, such as the motifs and the flowing or zigzag lines. Straight lines and outer borders can be added later with a ruler and light ballpoint line, when the main embroidery has been done. This gives much straighter lines, and also enables the worker to decide where any additional details are to be added. Exactly how much is put into a design is a matter of personal decision. When the main design has been worked, it may be thought better to vary the position of the final lines or to omit some of them altogether.

Opposite

Plate 2

a Miller wall panel 1   chart 4
b Ploughman magazine cover   charts 9 and 9a
c Child's sectional cap chart 11
d Pentagon ball   chart 10

6 Using templates

Cut-out shapes, usually called *templates*, can be traced and cut from firm paper or thin card, laid on the material and traced round many times or in many positions. They offer a simple way to put in more or less than is given on a chart, making it wider or narrower, larger or smaller. Thus there is scope for taking parts from an existing design, and creating, with very little drawing skill, quite a new design.

A template is also an extremely valuable guide for ensuring even stitches, lines and shapes. Zigzags can be kept sharply pointed and straight; wavy lines can flow regularly; scallops, circles, hearts and ovals can be kept true to shape.

Photograph *4* shows some of the templates which were used to make articles illustrated in this book. They could be traced directly from the photograph or from several of the charts in part 2.

Note the method of tracing round three identical coins to make a heart or round four to make an oval. To make larger or smaller hearts and ovals, use identical coins or counters in other sizes. To make circular motifs in different sizes, draw round a wineglass, a cup or a saucer. They can be given scalloped or serrated edges by folding them as in diagram *8d* and cutting away the edges as required. (See also page *41*.)

For zigzag feather stitch, a template is most useful in keeping outlines straight and stitches even. It is easily made from a postcard if small, or a grocery carton if larger. Either trace the shape from one of the charts, or work out zigzags of any size on squared paper. A few sheets of squared paper from a school arithmetic book are ideal for working out this and some of the following ideas.

Characteristic parts of many of the borders are the flowing and curving lines. A template for these can be traced from several of the charts, or worked out as shown in diagram *5*. Three or four coins of identical size can be arranged in different ways to produce many types of wavy borders. They are shown here laid against a straight line, but it would be easier to lay them on squared paper.

Photograph 4   Templates

Try out the four types as follows.

Diagram 5a   Lay the coins along a line, just touching the line and each other. Trace round them as shown, remove the coins, thus giving a deeply waved line which can be repeated as often as required to make a template.

Diagram 5b   Space the coins out evenly, trace round them. The curves are less deep and a slightly different shape.

Diagram 5c   Push the coins close together, so that they lie up and down alternately, and the waves are still less.

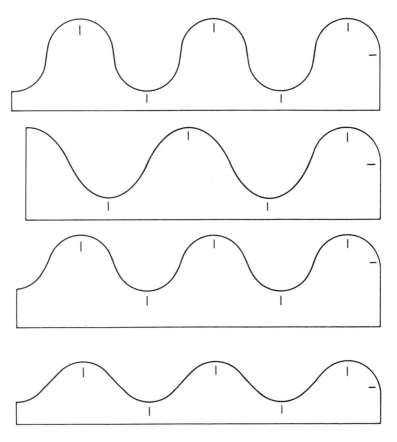

Diagram 5   Making curved borders

Diagram 5d   Emphasize the up-and-down position, giving a very shallow wave.

When the outlines are satisfactory, trace and cut out a template giving several repeats. Where coins are not large enough for the purpose, perhaps for a wide flowing border down a panel or round a skirt, cut out several paper 'counters' by tracing round a wineglass or saucer, and use these to build up the line. It is helpful to crease the counters into quarters, and to mark the divisions on the templates, as shown in the diagrams.

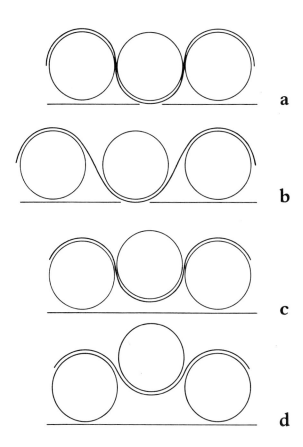

a

b

c

d

A scalloped, rather than a wavy line is sometimes required. A useful size for tracing is given in charts 3 and 9a. See also the *Ploughman* design, chapter 17, where a double scalloped edge is used on the magazine cover (colour plate 2).

Scallops of other sizes can be made as shown in diagram 6. Either use squared paper or draw two parallel lines fairly close together. Lay a coin or a larger counter along them and trace a scalloped line sufficient times to cut a template from it (diagram 6). Take care to keep the scallops quite shallow, for deep points are more difficult to work and less successful.

Before using a template, mark a straight guide line with tacking the full length of the area to be worked, and indicate, either with pins or a tacking stitch, the centre and other important points. Lay the template in place, hold it down very firmly, and trace lightly with a ballpoint pen along the shaped lines.

Avoid using a very long template, even where a long line is being marked, for it is difficult to hold accurately for tracing. The sizes given here are the most suitable. Trace the length of the template, lift it and move it along, taking care to 'key' it in place by matching short guide lines along the edges.

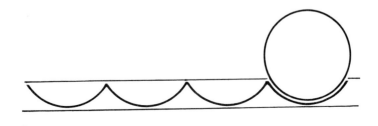

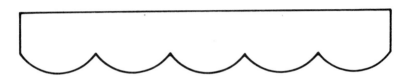

Diagram 6   Making a scalloped edge

7 Motifs, corners, squares and circles

There are many ways to use the straight borders shown on the charts, either copied or adapted. Later chapters give details and advice for making a variety of articles in this way. The illustrations show many items with such borders and some with the designs arranged to suit other shapes. Experienced embroiderers will have their own methods, but some suggestions are given here for those who need them.

Small motifs

Fourteen motifs are given in charts *11* and *12* and still more can be taken from the main charts. Chapter 18 gives details for using them on several articles. All that is needed is to trace those required, apply them to the fabric and work in appropriate stitches and colours.

If they are to be used singly, it is best to restrict their use to small objects, such as a pincushion, needle-book or cover for a powder compact. Where a number of small motifs are to be used on a larger article, such as a panel or a cushion, place them within some kind of framework (*wall panel* colour plate *2*, *square cushion* colour plate *3*). Avoid using in isolated positions such as the four corners of a mat, or in a single line along an apron, for they can look thin and spotty unless expertly planned.

Corners and squares

Although all the designs given here can be used just as they are in countless ways, there are occasions, for instance on cushions, mats and tablecloths, when corners or squares need to be planned (tablecloth centre photograph *10c*, square mat photograph *7a*, three mats photograph *5b*). These can be built up quite easily with the use of a mirror (diagram *7*).

An ordinary handbag mirror without a bevelled or framed edge can be employed for a first simple experiment as shown here. For wider borders, it is worth purchasing a larger unframed piece of mirror-glass from a glazier; a cheap off-cut will serve the purpose, as the exact size is not important.

To plan a corner, lay the chosen straight border flat on the table, and stand the mirror upright across it as shown in diagram *7a*. This will show you the detail of a corner. Still keeping the same angle, move the mirror backwards and forwards, thus lengthening or shortening the corner until the reflection gives the detail which seems best. Every border calls for different treatment and it is most interesting to try out various positions. Having decided on the best corner detail, draw a pencil line diagonally across the paper, using the lower edge of the mirror as a guide. The resulting angled ends of the straight border can then be used to build up one or more corners. Cut along the diagonal line. Reverse the tracing paper and fit the diagonal lines together as shown in diagram 7b. If the lines cannot be seen on the reversed side, retrace them.

When using a transfer, two diagonal ends must be cut in opposite directions in order to fit them together as shown in diagram 7b. Lay a strip of gummed paper, damped side up, on the table, fit the two angled ends of the tracing or transfer paper together and stick them down, cutting away the spare gummed paper.

Whole squares can be built up in this way. Sometimes, however, it is desirable to take an experimental look before cutting, to see what the finished square would look like in different positions. This can be done by placing two mirrors at right angles to each other, which will give a view of the complete square. For a preliminary try-out of several designs, to consider which one squares up best in the desired size, use two mirrors directly on the given charts.

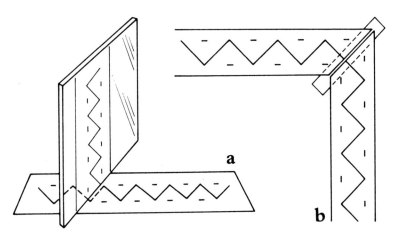

Diagram 7   Making a square

Circular designs

Photographs 3 and 8 show two circular shapes built up from straight borders. These and many others can be worked out with folded paper. The principle is similar in most cases, but it is worth trying it in its simplest form first (diagrams 8a and b). From thin tracing paper, cut a circle a little larger than the desired circular design, outlining it either with compasses or by drawing round a cup or glass. Use a small circle for a first experiment. A few more circles drawn within the outline make guides for placing the details. It will soon become clear where these are required. Fold the paper exactly into halves, then into smaller sections creasing them firmly (diagram 8a). On one section, trace a portion of the desired design. Open out the paper, and by folding and refolding, trade this section on to the remaining ones. Small and simple designs are easy to prepare. Diagram 8b shows the spiral pattern taken from chart 1c and used for the round mat in photograph 3. A larger or more involved design needs more thought. Diagram 8c shows how the tablecloth centre in photograph 8 was worked out, by folding a large circle into sections, and marking each one into parts. There is no need to use every line on the original pattern; select details as required.

Small flower shapes to be used as motifs can also be made in a similar way from paper circles as mentioned on page 34. Fold the circle into sections, mark and then cut out a scalloped or serrated edge, and cut away the centre if desired (diagram 8d). Open the paper and use it as a pattern to cut a cardboard template.

Other shapes

Not every design can be worked out by the mirror or paper folding methods. An oval or a rectangle may be required, or an individual shape such as the square mat in photograph 12c. In such cases, pencil out on plain paper the approximate size and shape required. On several separate pieces of thin tracing paper, trace the main elements of the straight border, each one several times. Cut roughly round the outer lines of each tracing, and lay them out experimentally in different positions within the boundary of the shape until the desired detail is obtained. Then trace the parts in place. An example of this method is explained in more detail in chapter 15.

When working out squares, circles or other shapes, it is usually best to build up the main elements over the entire shape. Then add inner and outer borders or other details where required. Curves,

a

b

d

c

Diagram 8   Circular designs from folded paper

zigzags and scallops can be traced from templates and added as well. Indeed, a shape can often be built up with templates alone. Consider how few, rather than how many lines or details are needed. An effect of rich stitchery may be desired, but a sparing use of well thought-out detail gives better results than a crowded and over-decorated piece of work.

If the paper is not too thick, the completed design can be placed on the material with a sheet of dressmakers' carbon paper in between, and traced as described in chapter 5. Otherwise, the design must first be marked out on tracing paper. In either case, it is advisable to press or mark with tacking on the material the centre lines down, across and diagonally, and rule corresponding lines on the paper, so that the placing is accurate.

Where a design is large or very detailed such as that in photograph 8 it is sometimes better to do a section at a time, rather than tracing the whole shape on to the material. This demands accurate marking out of the divisions on the material, but gives a good result on a large surface, and is less tiring than dealing with a very large tracing. For this method, make a tracing of a section of the design; apply it to a similar section of the material; then lift the paper and repeat on all the remaining sections. Take care that each section matches exactly.

Where templates have been used experimentally to build up all or part of the design, they can be used again to apply the details to the material.

8 Hems, edges and finishes

Where the needlewoman's interest is mainly in the embroidery, keep the finishing processes to a minimum or dispense with them altogether. A cushion or an apron could be made up by machine, a panel quickly finished with purchased braid or fringe. An embroidered border might be worked on a plain skirt, a colourful band of stitchery added to a schoolgirl's hairband or a child's ready-made dress. Whilst such items may not win prizes or become heirlooms, they can afford satisfaction and practical use. Sometimes items completed in this way can be more effective than with indifferent hand-finishing.

Many needlewomen, however, take pleasure and pride in a high standard of hand-finishing to set off their embroidery. The usual dressmaking or fine sewing processes will be familiar to these women or can be followed from any standard book on sewing. Those used in the articles illustrated are mentioned in the following paragraphs. Further information is given with each article described in later chapters.

1   On fairly fine material, a quick and good edging is made by working a line of feather stitching on *single* fabric, then turning a hem to the wrong side and sewing it down so that the embroidery covers the hemming. (*Long runner* photograph *6c, long mat* photograph *12b, three mats* colour plate *1, place mat* colour plate *4*.)

2   Another good method is to finish the edge with hem-stitching, using embroidery thread related to the main colour scheme. On a wide hem this gives weight, and is especially satisfactory on table mats and chairbacks. It will keep trim and shapely through the constant laundering such items need (diagram *2e, chairbacks* photographs *10b* and *11d, square mat* photograph *12c*).

3   A mat or runner often looks better with the interest centred on the embroidery, with no visible edge stitching (*mats* in photograph *5b, square mat* photograph *7a, long mat* photograph *11a*). Where it is backed with interlining, this is easily arranged as follows. On all edges of the mat, turn a single narrow fold to the wrong side. Trim the interlining evenly all round so that it covers the raw edges of the fold, but lies just within the outer border of the mat. With fine sewing cotton, fell the raw edge of the interlining to the fold, taking care not to take the stitches through to the front.

4 With coarse linen or other heavy fabric, ordinary hems can look clumsy. On such material, also sides of panels and chairbacks and on circular mats or tablecloths, the edges are better finished with bias binding. (*Tablecloth* photograph *8* and *chairbacks* photographs *10b* and *11d*.) Only a narrow single turning need be allowed for this method, but ensure that this is the edging to be used before leaving such a small allowance. Lay the bias binding and the raw edge of the material exactly together, right sides inwards, and stitch them along the crease in the binding (diagram *9a*). Turn the binding over to the wrong side of the material, and hem down, preferably behind a line of embroidery (diagram *9b*).

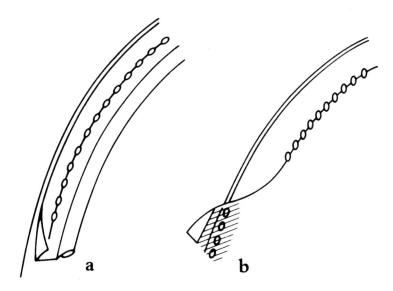

Diagram 9   Finishing edges with bias binding

5   A cushion cover should be slightly smaller than its pad. The simplest way to make up the cover is to join front and back all round with a single seam. For a more shapely result, insert a covered piping cord or a narrow double frill into the seam. Alternatively, make a single seam and trim it with cord, braid or fringe, taking care that these will stand up to the hard wear which a cushion usually receives.

6   When planning the design on a flat piece of material remember that a cushion is plump when in use, and when finished, the interest will be concentrated on the centre. Therefore it is best to avoid embroidering an elaborate border round the edges. Either it will get lost to the eye as the cushion edges recede, or, if very bold, it will draw the interest away from the main design.

Part 2

The previous chapters give general guidance on embroidery as specially applying to the designs in this book.

The following chapters give specific suggestions for using the charts.

It has been thought helpful to mention the colours and fabric used for each of the articles illustrated.

Most embroiderers will no doubt translate the colours and fabrics used here into details of their own choice, giving a more lively and spontaneous effect, and showing their own personality in the finished item. Some useful and successful stitches have been indicated on the charts. Here again, the individual worker may like to try out different ones, either to aim at a new effect, or because she enjoys doing one stitch more than another.

The earlier designs will possibly be found the quickest and easiest to work, with the later ones calling for more time and skill. Favourite stitches and patterns are sure to be chosen at random from the charts, and their details can be added, omitted or combined.

9 Three narrow borders chart *1*

These borders are planned for use where a minimum of embroidery is required. While allowing for personal taste, they offer an opportunity to try out this type of work for the first time, or to obtain an attractive effect quickly.

Each border can be used alone, perhaps to give a touch of hand stitchery to a hair band, a belt or a machine-made garment, or as an additional outer border on another design. The three can also be used together to build up a wide border (*apron* photograph *5c*).

Border A is very versatile. By cutting a template and outlining it as required, it can be used to follow either a straight line or a broad curve (*child's pinafore dress* photograph *5a*).

Border B is a familiar deep zigzag shape, smaller than those found in some of the later charts. It is worked in feather stitch, with the short detached lines in whipped chain. Aim to make very sharp turns on the points. To do this in feather stitch, take one extra stitch quite upright on each point.

Border C is shown here in its small and simple form, but variations of this spiral design appear on many patterns. In chart *1* a straight edging is given, but this may be omitted if desired. Variations can be seen in photographs *3* and *7*, and colour plate *2*, also in charts *9* and *9a*. It forms an important part of the decoration on the magazine cover (colour plate *2*) and the workbag (colour plate *4*). In a simpler form, it is shown on the fold-over bag (photograph *7b*) and as a circular border on a mat (photograph *3*).

The spirals look best when worked in whipped blanket stitch, beginning always in the centre of the spiral and working outwards. Note that on *border C* the small shapes lie up and down alternately. Begin at the right hand end of the border in the centre of the first spiral, and blanket stitch round to the open end. Then take the needle through to the back, pass the thread to the centre of the next spiral, and repeat. Notice, however, that because the spirals curve alternately, the working thread must be thrown to the right of the needle for one, to the left of the needle for the next. To whip the stitching, work in the same order, whipping each spiral on the surface, then taking the thread along the back to the next one.

48   (*overleaf*) Chart 1   Three borders

a Drayman cushion   chart 3
b Square cushion   charts 11 and 12

Plate 3

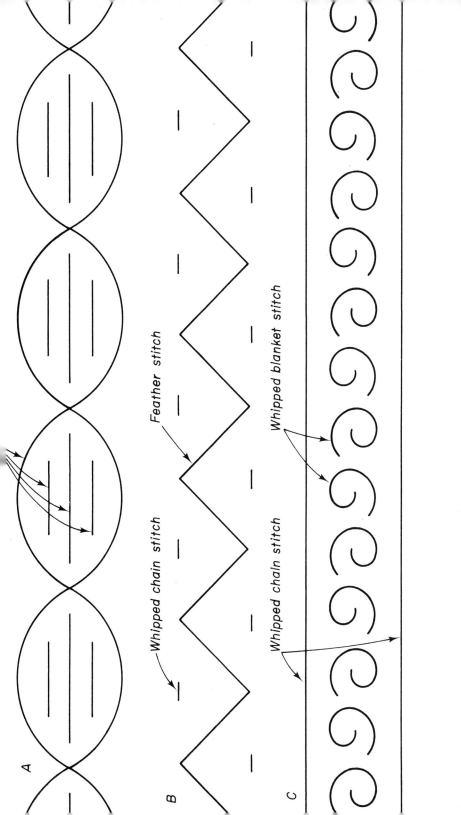

A

B

Feather stitch

Whipped chain stitch

C

Whipped blanket stitch

Whipped chain stitch

Child's pinafore dress   photograph 5*a*

A bold scheme of black, white and candy pink is used on a grey flannel dress made from a trade pattern. To ensure an accurate running border round neck and along hem, the shoulder and side seams were stitched and the border marked out by using a template. Then the embroidery was worked and pressed, and the dress completed. A purchased dress could be used if care were taken to stitch only through single fabric.

Three place mats   photograph 5*b*

These show each border used in a square, building up the details first on paper with the aid of a mirror (diagram 7). Dark tones of rather coarse linen are used, stitched entirely in white.

A backing of *vilene* is used on each mat, giving substance to the work and providing a lining. Tack it behind the linen in different directions, as shown on the lowest, unfinished mat (photograph 5*b*), leaving the edges free. Work the embroidery through both thicknesses, remove tacking threads and press well. Complete the edge as described on page *44*.

Silver grey apron   photograph 5*c*

Two greens and white are used on pale grey cotton, with all three borders making one wide one. A short strip of *border C* is set upright at each end to make extra width, with a tiny echo of the spirals worked on the ends of the ties, and a length of *border A* on the waistband. The side and lower borders are outlined in deep green ridged braid, fly stitched in white (diagram *3a*). Two smocked panels hold the waist fulness, but pleats or gathers would serve the purpose equally well. Work all the embroidery before making up the apron.

Photograph 5   Three narrow borders
     a   child's pinafore dress
     b   three place mats
     c   silver-grey apron

10 Waggoner design chart *2*

This wider border, with its hint of winding roads and wheels, is an open and quickly worked design. It offers scope for simple but effective colour schemes. The same main stitches have been used on all the articles shown in photograph *6* and the mat photograph *7a*. The long wavy lines are worked in feather stitch and the small wheel shapes in blanket stitch, sometimes whipped, sometimes not. Different fabrics, colours and arrangements have produced four very different results.

Teacosy   photograph *6a*

A very fine, soft, deep red woollen fabric is used for this, backed with *vilene* to give more body, and stitched with primrose and two shades of green. An interesting effect is gained by using two very close shades of green on the long feather stitched lines, and stitching in the lighter green and whipping with the darker one on the inner circle of the wheels. The outer circles of the wheels are stitched and whipped in the primrose shade.

Measure for size and turnings required, cut out material a little larger, and mark the exact shape of the finished cosy cover with tacking. Back with interlining if required. Plan and apply a sufficient length of design across the lower part, rounding off the curves at each end and adding a few lines if necessary to fill in the width (photograph *6a*). Complete the embroidery and cut the material to shape, also preparing a reverse side, either plain or with a different design (photograph *11b*). Work a single chain stitch line round the curved edges, and join the sides either with a plain seam or a covered piping cord. Turn in and hem the lower edges, inserting a pad of foam or wadding.

Striped apron   photograph *6b*

White cotton striped in pale gold makes an effective background for stitchery in bright gold and chocolate brown. As suggested for the teacosy, the long lines are feather stitched in brown and whipped in a slightly darker shade, with the same plan used for the wheel shapes in gold blanket stitch with deeper gold whipping.

Some thought is required to make good use of a striped background, and here the fabric has been used crosswise for the border.

Photograph 6   Waggoner design
      a   teacosy
      b   striped apron
      c   long runner

To do this, cut a length from one selvedge, work the embroidery along it, and stitch it across the lower part of the apron.

Long runner   photograph *6c*

Like the other mats illustrated (*Shepherd* photograph *12b* and *c* and *Milkmaid* photograph *11a*) this was planned for use in contemporary style beneath plate glass on sideboard, dressing table or long coffee table. Simplicity and good colour contrast make for success. The fabric is raspberry-pink, the stitchery mainly in black, with a little white and just a touch of scarlet. The wavy lines are worked in feather stitch, with the short straight lines in whipped chain, all in black. The wheel shapes have an interesting treatment (diagram *10*, expanded for clarity). Work an outer circle of whipped blanket stitch in black. As closely as possible within it, work a circle of scarlet stem stitch. Work the smaller circle with white whipped blanket stitch, scarlet stem stitch within it, and fill the centre with black satin stitch. This method of filling in can be used with advantage for many other types of motif. The runner is finished with a single line of feather stitch at the edges, with turnings hemmed down beneath the stitching.

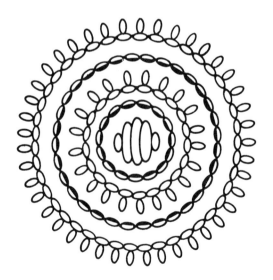

Diagram 10   Waggoner motif

Square mat   photograph 7a

This matches the long runner, using the same stitches and colours.
The design is an example of squaring up a straight border by using
a mirror (see pages 39 and 40).

Photograph 7   Designs from various charts
a   Waggoner square mat
b   Ploughman fold-over bag
c   Gardener round pincushion
d   Wheelwright spectacle case

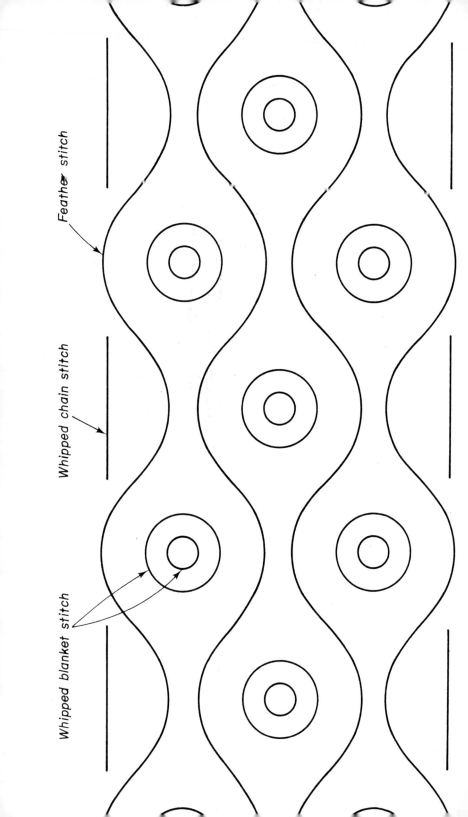

Feather stitch

Whipped chain stitch

Whipped blanket stitch

Stitch detail of Waggoner design

◀ Chart 2   Waggoner

11 **Drayman** chart 3

This is a versatile design, with traditional motifs and borders used to make a pleasing modern decoration. The two trial pieces in photograph 3 indicate some stitch and colour experiments, which were then used in different ways.

Place mat colour plate 4 facing page 65

A fairly coarse crash in sky blue has the main lines and motifs in white. Deep blue is used for the large zigzag lines, and short lines in still deeper blue fill in the leaf centres and the links of the border.

Some variations in the leaf centres are given in diagram 11 and on the trial pieces. A single line of whipped chain, a few feather stitches increasing in size or a solid filling of satin stitch could be used effectively on these and other similar motifs. Where the space is small, the filling should be light and uncrowded.

Two-colour cushion colour plate 3 facing page 48

Here a similar design takes on a completely different appearance, using a central contrast panel and some variation in the width and arrangement of the border. Sailcloth in natural colour and deep burnt orange is worked entirely in black. The width of the panel in relation to the complete shape should be worked out on paper. Make a fairly long tracing of the main design and two separate tracings of the narrow twisted border. Lay them on the trial paper to plan the proportion of the parts, and decide where it is best to centre the design in order to cover the area satisfactorily.

Stitches used are similar to those on the placemat, except that the leaf centres are filled in with satin stitch. The work could be arranged in two ways. Either the embroidery could be worked on three separate strips and then seamed together, or the seaming done first and then the embroidery. In either case, take care to make straight, firm seams. Avoid embroidering exactly on the seam lines, as this tends to weaken the seaming. The cushion shown here was made up with a plain back and a piped edge, both in self colour.

Circular tablecloth photograph 8

This was made to fit a round coffee table, with the design just filling in the table surface and a narrow border at the outer edge. Thus the

58

main decoration appears on the flat top where it is seen most, and the edges, falling into folds, carry a minimum of decoration.

Pale blue linen was used for the cloth, with the embroidery in black, two blues and a little primrose yellow. The design is a more detailed one, but gives scope for personal planning and colour sense. It has already been used as an example of arranging colour and of making a circular design (pages *17* and *41*, diagram *8*). Note how the main design is defined by using black on the outer edge, working through to the palest blue in the inner parts. The light yellow, used with whipped chain within the links of the borders, gives a pleasing highlight. A hem round the outer edge would look clumsy here, and is not needed as the weight of the folds make the cloth hang well. Instead, the edge is very simply neatened with bias binding (chapter 8 and diagram *9*).

Photograph 8   Drayman circular tablecloth

Whipped chain stitch, feathered on outer curves

Whipped chain stitch

Stitch detail of Drayman design

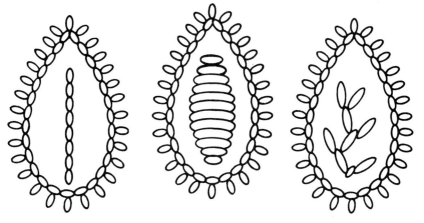

Diagram 11   Drayman motifs

◀ Chart 3   Drayman

12 **Miller** chart 4

Curves and angles blend in this design to make a pattern which can be varied in width, detail and colour. Note the contrasting styles in the articles illustrated: fine stitching in pastel shades on a child's dress (photograph 9); a simple decoration on a place mat (colour plate 1), a bold effect on a wall panel (colour plate 2).

The stitches used on each item are almost identical in each case. Photograph 3 shows a small panel which was tried out first, to experiment with detail and colour.

Child's sleeveless dress   photograph 9

This was cut from a trade pattern, slightly adapted, and was made entirely by hand. The same general idea could be carried out on any similar garment, purchased or made at home. The design would look well on a sun dress with gathered skirt, bib and shoulder-straps in the style shown in photograph 13a. The dress shown here is made from very fine shell-pink poplin, embroidered with coton-à-broder in white and three shades of pink. The inner motifs are white, working through medium pinks to the deepest one, which is used for the straight boundary lines, the lowest line of the border and the zigzag feather stitch on the bodice.

The dressmaking processes were carefully planned first, then carried out when all the stitchery was completed, with handmade buttons in the same threads to give a final touch.

Blue place mat   colour plate 1 facing page 16

This is one of a set of four mats using the design very simply along the two ends. Fine linen in fresh, clear, pastel shades is used, with the designs worked mainly in white, with small amounts of colour echoing the linen colours. For the blue mat, the deepest blue is used for solid satin stitch centres in the half circles, but the leaf centres are left empty. Neat hems, carefully mitred at the corners, are stitched down beneath the outer zigzag borders.

Wall panel   colour plate 2 facing page 33

This is in striking contrast to the other uses for this design, and shows how a traditional border can be suited to contemporary taste. A thick black embroidery thread is used throughout, with the stitches already mentioned. The main difference is that instead of repeating

62

raph 9   Miller design for child's sleeveless dress

the four-leaf motif within the diamond border, two motifs of trees and sails taken from charts *11* and *12* have been used alternately, with the diamonds slightly bowed outwards to give more space. The background is light-weight embroidery felt, backed with iron-on *vilene*. One colour only could be used, but the effect is heightened here by stripes of brilliant flame, pink and lime green. Plan the length and width of the panel on paper first, considering the number of pattern repeats so that they will terminate completely at top and bottom. Allow for a narrow turning down each side, and sufficient at top and bottom for the desired mounting. The panel shown here has short lengths of wooden curtain rod slotted through top and bottom hems, but more elaborate 'bell-pull' fitments can be purchased.

If stripes are to be used, try out the widths to get the most effective proportions. Here the three stripes were actually the same width, but the side turnings taken under on the two outside stripes have made these narrower and give an added width to the centre stripe. Try to avoid the straight boundary lines lying exactly on the joins; it is more effective to have them slightly beyond the centre stripe.

Cut the long felt edges very straight, preferably marking the cutting lines first against a long ruler. The felt can be joined along the raw edges, but for greater firmness and ease of stitching, iron the *vilene* to each separate felt stripe; then trim it carefully to the exact edges.

The two joining seams on this panel have been worked with the zigzag attachment on the sewing machine. They could also be oversewn with thick sewing cotton by hand.

Work the embroidery in black or a very dark colour, using the tree and sail motifs or any others preferred. A thick thread will give the best results, but it does mean simplifying the detail as much as possible so that the parts of the pattern are clearly defined. Press the work on the wrong side, but **without damping.** Turn under a fold along each long edge, and catch it down to the wrong side with fine cotton. Make a hem at top and bottom, and insert a length of wooden rod in each. Work a large ring with very close blanket stitch, and sew it very securely to the centre of the top edge. If preferred, use a purchased fitment for top and bottom, or use fringe or braid, but avoid details which draw attention away from the main design.

(overleaf) Chart 4 Miller

Plate 4

a Drayman place mat   chart 3
b Ploughman workbag   chart 9

Feather stitch

Whipped blanket stitch

13   Wheelwright   chart 5

This is a closely worked design, allowing for considerable variety of stitches and arrangements. The four articles illustrated bear this out. The pink place mat in colour plate *1* shows very simple stitchery in white and a little colour, while the three articles in photograph *10*, each made by a different worker, show contrasting stitches and results.

Many combinations of stitch and colour are possible. Brief details are given here, and the exact stitches used in each case can be observed from photographs *3* and *10* and colour plate *1*

With so many possibilities, it is best to keep an open mind until experiments have been made. Either work a trial piece (photograph *3*), or start on the actual article by working the main parts in colours and stitches which seem reasonably certain. It is then more satisfactory to fill in the final details to give weight and definition to the entire design.

The *Wheelwright* design is used on the spectacle case in photograph *7*. Directions are given in chapter 18, page *87*.

Blue apron   photograph *10a*

Here the effect relies for success on strong colour and contrast on a soft blue cotton fabric. The worker has concentrated on the border, with a minimum of decoration on other parts of the apron. Two well-defined blues, deep hyacinth and lighter forget-me-not, are mainly used, with accents of deep gold and pale primrose yellow. Instead of using deeper colour to add weight to the lower part of the border, an equally good effect is obtained by omitting the double zigzag at the upper edge, but retaining it with the addition of an extra line along the lower edge.

Chairback   photograph *10b*

This is one of a set of four, each with a different design. (Another shown in photograph *11d*.) The fabric is fine pale yellow linen, with the embroidery in black, crimson and bright gold.

When planning such an article, allow for fairly deep hems on every side, to keep them firm and good throughout frequent laundering. The lower front hem should be especially wide and firmly finished.

Photograph 10   Wheelwright design
      a   blue apron
      b   chairback
      c   tablecloth centre

Having decided on the exact width of the side hems, work a line of feather stitch down each side, planning and working the border to repeat exactly between them. A second feather stitch line down each side, a good distance in from the first ones, and finishing where it meets the border, adds strength to the sides.

The hems can be turned under and caught down beneath the feather stitching at sides and back edge, or finished with a bias binding (diagram 9). The lower front hem is secured here with a line of hem stitching (diagram 2e) which makes a very strong edge, but it could be feather stitched if preferred.

Tablecloth centre   photograph 10c

The illustration shows the centre of a large white tablecloth, with the interest concentrated on the centre square motif. Details, colouring and stitches have been planned for a bold effect. The square was worked out with mirrors (pages 39 and 40 and diagram 7).

Colours used were vivid scarlet and buttercup yellow with a very little black. The stitching is very close, with strong contrast between the wide, flowing feather stitch on the light-edged circles and the close blanket stitch, turning inwards and in some parts interlocking, on the dark-edged ones (photograph 2a). The formal outer and inner borders are worked entirely in scarlet, except that the straight chain stitch lines are whipped with yellow. The outer edge of the cloth is very simply finished with the same type of border.

Pink place mat   colour plate 1 facing page 16

One of a matching set of mats, this is worked mainly in white, with small amounts of two pinks on fine linen in deep pastel pink. Note that the circular motifs have been slightly reduced and the fillings simplified, to avoid an overcrowded effect on the limited area of the borders. On a larger mat, the design could be used full sized.

Whipped chain stitch

Satin stitch

Feather stitch

Whipped blanket stitch

14 Milkmaid chart 6

In the original embroideries, the heart motif appears often in bands and squares of closely packed stitchery. Here a simplified border has been worked out to suit present day requirements. It can be used exactly as given, or easily varied in width and detail. A well shaped heart can be made in any size by using three coins (photograph 4) and three different fillings are given, one on the articles in photograph 11 and two others in the motifs on chart 11. The wide zigzag enclosing the heart motifs could be made in any size and spacing by using a card template as in photograph 4.

All the articles use the given border in a similar way, and the stitches are almost identical, but background fabric and colour of threads have produced varying results (photograph 11).

Long mat photograph 11a

Lime green linen is used for this, with all the embroidery in dark wine red. It was backed with light-weight *vilene*. On such a design as this, an outer border is best avoided. The mat can be finished at the edges as described on page 44.

Teacosy photograph 11b

This is the reverse side of the cosy shown on photograph 6. General making-up directions are given on page 52. A similar fine woollen fabric is used, but for this side a light emerald green background has the design worked in three shades of red, from light geranium to deep crimson. Thus the two sides are complementary.

Zipped bag photograph 11c

This is in navy blue felt, with stitching and the zipper in sky blue. Instead of trying to hide the zipper, make it the focal point of the embroidery, adapting the detail slightly as required. The bag illustrated is suitable for evening use or for holding handkerchieves, but the idea could be carried out in other sizes and fabrics, with the zipper placed in any position, perhaps to serve as a nightdress or pyjama case or a hot water bottle cover. The secret of easy making up is the order of work. Cut two identical pieces of fabric (in this case, felt backed with *vilene*) and on one piece plan the position of the zipper. Mark the position with a straight line. Leave room for

Photograph 11   Milkmaid design
      a   long mat
      b   teacosy
      c   zipped bag
      d   chairback

Whipped blanket stitch

Whipped chain stitch

Zigzag feather stitch

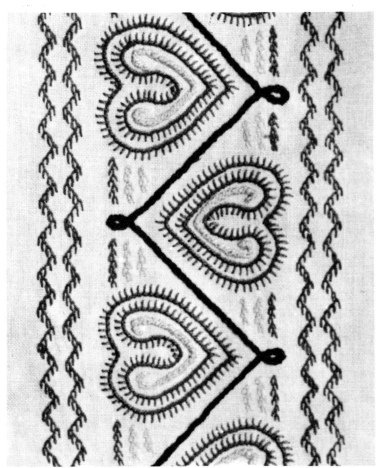

Stitch detail of Milkmaid design

whatever turnings will be needed, and plan and work the embroidery. Press the work, cut along the line and sew in the zipper by hand or machine. Lay both bag pieces together, trim them to the same size, and either bind the four sides or join them with blanket stitch.

Chairback   photograph *11d*

This is one of the set referred to on pages *66* and *68* where general making-up directions are given. The wide looped zigzag is worked in black, the V-shaped heart centres and the two inner of the three short lines in gold, and the rest in crimson.

15 Shepherd chart 7

The repeat of this design is longer than usual, giving more scope for using the spiral shepherd's crook motif. This motif also provides easier spacing on different articles, such as three across a cushion, five on a long runner, two on a teacosy or a larger number round the border of a skirt. The stitches can be clearly observed from photograph 12, and they should be studied and perhaps tried out first, for some are used in an unusual way. The large double-ended spiral needs to be worked in two halves. Begin working the blanket stitch in one spiral centre, go as far as the middle of the joining line, and fasten off. Begin again at the other spiral centre, and continue until the second line of stitching meets the first one in the middle. When whipping the stitches, begin at the centres each time and work to the middle line.

The smaller double-ended spirals on the square mat are worked in a similar manner to the large ones. The very small single spirals are worked from the centres outwards. Other stitch details are suggested on chart 7. Note the feathered chain on the outer curves of each motif, which gives an attractive finish (diagram 1d).

Oblong cushion photograph 12a

Heavy sky-blue crash is stitched entirely in rather thick white embroidery thread. Three repeats fit well along a small cushion, or four would fill the space on a larger sized one. The outer curves of the design have been extended to make a straight line border round the cushion, with another line outside it. Make up the cushion with a plain back, and either a single seam or a self-covered piping cord to join the two sides.

Two matching mats photograph 12b and c

Both of these are worked entirely in black on a background of magenta heavyweight furnishing cotton. The long mat uses five repeats of the pattern, with a single line of feather stitch round the edge. The square mat has a hem-stitched edge. The design on the square mat has an interesting shape which was determined by the arrangement of the large spirals. As already mentioned on pages 41 and 43, this was arrived at after experiments with cut-out shapes on tracing paper. Four tracings of the double-ended spiral were made and roughly cut out, then laid out experimentally on plain

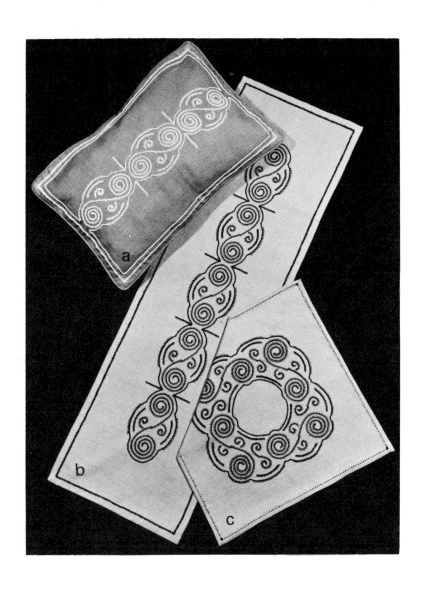

Photograph 12 Shepherd design
    a   oblong cushion
    b and c   two matching mats

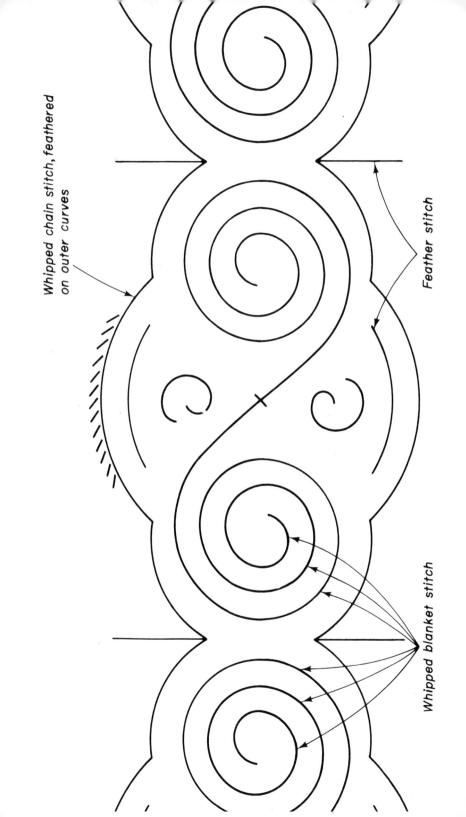

Whipped chain stitch, feathered on outer curves

Feather stitch

Whipped blanket stitch

paper until they fell into the approximate size required for the mat. When satisfactorily positioned, they were traced on to the paper and an outer and inner border were added. This follows the outlines of the spirals, yet keeps fairly close to the shape of the border on the original design. Further details were added, again very similar to the originals, to fill in the spaces.

Stitch detail of Shepherd design

16 Gardener chart 8

Variations of this design, with its hint of flowers and winding paths, were used in many English counties in the past. It is simple and attractive enough to be used today almost in its original form. Different fillings for the flowers can be worked, and if those on chart 8 and photograph 13 and colour plate 1 are not liked, others can be taken from charts 11 and 12. The stitches are mainly similar on the articles in photograph 13.

Child's sun dress   photograph 13a

It can be made without a pattern, as it consists solely of straight pieces. This dress is in turquoise blue cotton, with the embroidery worked in strongly contrasting black, white and tangerine.

Having determined the size required, cut a piece for the skirt, and double lengths for bib, waistband and shoulder-straps. Plan the skirt to join down centre back, and apply the design well up from the lower edge to allow for a deep hem.

Work the skirt border, adding a straight instead of a zigzag boundary line if desired. On one half of the bib, work a short related panel, and fold the other half back to make a lining.

Join the centre back seam, making a placket at the upper end. Gather the skirt into the double waistband, add bib and shoulder-straps, and fasten back waist with a button.

Summer skirt   photograph 13b

This can also be made without a pattern, being a straight length gathered into a band. The border would be suitable for any other skirt. The skirt shown here is washable rayon strawcloth in lime green. The stitchery is almost entirely in bright royal blue with just a touch of lighter blue. The stitches are mostly the same as on the sun dress, except that the blanket stitch outlining the flowers has been turned inwards and the detached chain omitted. Waistband and pocket have a narrow spiral border taken from chart 1c.

Green place mat   colour plate 1 facing page 16

This is one of the set of mats prepared and made up as described on page 62. Almond green linen is stitched mainly in white with two shades of deep green. As the length is limited, the design has been

Photograph 13   Gardener design
          a   child's sun dress
          b   summer skirt

Whipped blanket stitch

Zigzag feather stitch

adapted in proportion to a closer winding border and smaller flowers. Small centres from chart 5 have been used in the flower centres instead of the spiral and detached chain. Templates for the flowers and the winding border could be cut as described on pages 34 to 37 and in diagrams 5 and 8.

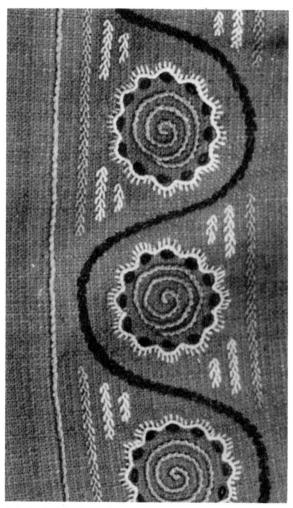

Stitch detail of Gardener design

17 **Ploughman** charts 9 and 9a

The symbolic seed of life motif appears in many patterns. Here it is combined with double spiral borders to make a design specially suited to run downwards, as for bags, panels or covers for books or magazines. A simpler design, using only a narrow part of the border, also looks well running across a small article such as the fold-over bag in photograph 7b. Many other variations would be possible by combining the details on charts 9 and 9a.

It is a good plan to work a trial piece, using the different parts and experimenting with stitches and colours, or even deciding which way up the design looks better. Such a piece is shown in photograph 3 from which the exact stitches can be observed in use. The seed shapes are shown with a double outline, but their details and fillings could be taken from diagrams 10 and 11 if preferred. Compare the spiral borders in this pattern with those shown on chart 1c and described on page 48. Note that the method of working is similar, but the right and left arrangement of the spirals is different.

Fold-over bag   photograph 7b

This uses the simplest form of the design. To prepare it, trace the spiral border from chart 9a, adding double or single scallops. Lay the tracing over chart 9, fitting the spirals in place, and trace off a zigzag border, or other details as desired.

In its simplest form the bag is a straight strip with the lower part folded up to make a deep pocket. Gussets can be added at the sides, or the bag made in any size, small for an evening handbag, larger for a pyjama case. The bag shown here is made from grosgrain fabric, black with a scarlet lining, and the stitchery is in white. If stiffened with an interlining, the flap falls easily in place, but a zipper or other fastening can be added if required.

Workbag   colour plate 4 facing page 65

Here the full design is used as on chart 9. The material is heavy sail-cloth, tomato red with almond green lining. For a bag which might be expected to carry a fair weight of knitting or sewing, very strong material, both for the outside and the lining, is essential, and a *vilene* interlining would add greater firmness.

82

Plan the making-up details before beginning the work, so that exact size and shape can be determined, and turnings allowed on every edge for a suitable finish. Cut the outer and inner parts to identical size, marking the curved side edges on both pieces, but leaving them uncut at this stage. Work the embroidery in colours related to the lining. Here the seed motifs and outer zigzags match the pale green lining, with the seed centres and inner zigzags in white, and the spiral borders in dark bottle green.

When the embroidery is completed and pressed, cut out the curved sides of the bag and its lining. Seam the straight sides and lower edges on each part separately. Place lining inside bag and tack together along the curved edges. Either finish them with a covered piping cord to add firmness, or turn the raw edges into face, and slipstitch together.

Magazine cover   colour plate *2* facing page *33*

This is a stiffened cover intended to hold a periodical. It has a foundation of two sheets of stiff card, joined along the spine with strong adhesive tape, covered with dark green furnishing cotton outside and lined with lemon yellow. The embroidered panel combines the main elements from chart *9* with the scalloped border from chart *9a*. To prepare it, trace the leaf and spiral details from chart *9*, lay the tracing on chart *9a*, fitting the spirals in place, and trace the double scalloped border and a boundary line on each side.

Cut the outer covering material with a very generous turning on all edges, and plan and work the panel so that it fits exactly the length of the cardboard foundation. Colours used here are almost entirely bright lemon yellow, with white for the outer scallops on each side and the leaf centres, and a fine line of rust-red stem stitch within the inner borders of the leaf motifs.

To make up the cover, lay the material very centrally on the cardboard, turn the edges on to the inside, and either stick them to the cardboard or secure them tightly by long, strong lacing stitches. Firm fitting is essential, but allowance must also be made for the cover to fold flat. Cut a lining with a turning on all edges, turn this under, and fell in place with small stitches lying just inside the cover. A length of strong elastic inside the fold of the cover will allow the periodical to be slipped in place.

Whipped blanket stitch

Zigzag feather stitch

Stitch detail of Ploughman design

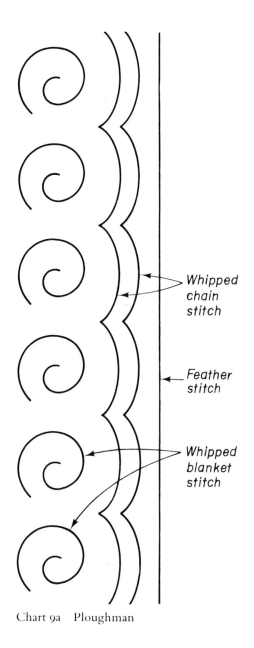

Whipped
chain
stitch

Feather
stitch

Whipped
blanket
stitch

Chart 9a   Ploughman

86

18   Miscellaneous motifs   charts *11* and *12*

This chapter collects some items briefly mentioned earlier in the book, and gives ideas and instructions for some well-tried favourites which appear always to be in demand for gifts or bazaars. Each item could be made in ways determined by the taste and skill of the worker and the materials available. For success, avoid overdecoration and aim for bright contrasting colours, firm fabrics and bold stitchery, good making up and finishing. Felt is used for most of the items shown here, but other materials could be used.

A very large variety of decorative motifs form part of the old border patterns. Some are symbolic, such as the heart and the seed of life. Others are taken from the wearer's trade, and thus we have windmill sails, wheels and trees. Some are doubtless copied or evolved from familiar objects or geometrical shapes. The charts *1* to *9* include a number of these motifs, and some others, interesting enough to be used without borders, are given in charts *11* and *12*.

Definite stitches cannot be given for embroidering each motif, but close observation of the illustrations will give ideas, and individual suggestions for using them are given in the following pages.

Round pincushion   photograph *7c*

A single motif within a circle or square provides a setting for a small, quickly worked article. It might be a pin cushion, a needle book, a tiny sewing case for travelling or a cover for a powder compact. Almost any motif could be worked in ways already suggested, but the pincushion in photograph *7c* gives a fresh idea for working a flower motif in felt appliqué. Two circles of firm card and two of bright-coloured felt are needed, with a few felt scraps in contrasting shades and a little black or very dark embroidery thread. Use a bold flower shape with large clear outlines rather than small details.

Cutting out accurate felt shapes from a paper pattern is not easy, but the following method is quick and good. Lay a piece of iron-on *vilene* over the motif, and trace with a ballpoint pen the separate shapes, for instance one tracing of the scallop-edge flower and one plain small circle for the centre. Cut out each one roughly, lay on the appropriate coloured felt, adhesive side down, and press with a warm iron. Cut round the ballpoint outline, thus giving an accurate shape and a firm edge into which to sew.

Tack the shapes to the background and attach them by working round the edges with any suitable stitches. Lay the two felt circles over the card ones, oversew all round, and insert pins into the edges.

Spectacle case   photograph 7d

A little stitchery, closely worked on any plain fabric, makes this simple shape into a decorative item. This case is worked with motifs taken from the wheelwright design (chart 5) in black, white and orange on grass-green felt, with a border of white ric-rac braid.

Cut a paper pattern to the desired size, outline it twice on a piece of felt but do not cut out the shapes. Tack a piece of heavy-weight interlining behind the shapes, and embroider through both thicknesses, using any desired motifs, simplified to suit the small area. A ric-rac border gives a quick, rich finish (pages 25 and 26 and diagram 3). Cut out the two shapes and join them with small firm stitches over the raw edge, stitching each side of the opening separately. Add a fastening just inside the opening, either a press stud or a short strip of *velcro* touch and close fastening.

Child's sectional cap   colour plate 2 facing page 33

Two different heart motifs from chart 11, alternating round six sections edged with ric-rac braid, make this cap. It was cut from a trade pattern, but a good one can be made by drawing round an ordinary electric iron, cutting out four or six paper sections, tacking them together, and adjusting them to fit the head. White, grass-green and black are used on a background of raspberry-pink woollen fabric.

Prepare each section separately. On frayable fabrics, allow turnings and tack them down over interlining shapes cut from the pattern. For felt, no turnings are needed on the upper curved edges, but allow a fold round the lower edge.

First attach the braid round the two upper edges of each section, using the method on pages 25 and 26 and diagram 3, or any other desired. Secure the outer edge of the braid with fairly close blanket stitch, with the line of loops lying exactly on the edge of the fabric. Mark out and work a heart motif on the lower part of each section.

Join the sections by whipping each pair of edges together over the loops of the blanket stitch. Turn under and hem the lower edge all round, covering the inner edge with a strip of strong straight-grained tape to keep it shapely in use.

Square cushion   colour plate *3* facing page *48*

This is an adventurous, quick and successful decoration for a cushion of any shape or size. Many ways of arranging and embroidering the motifs are possible; and square, oblong or even round cushions could be divided to make a well balanced arrangement from the separate units. Here a square of moss green furnishing fabric is divided into a diamond-shaped grid with ric-rac braid in emerald for the outer border, pale water-green inside. The motifs are boldly worked in thick threads, using many shades of parchment, gold, flame and green.

Plan the outer frame and inner divisions and mark the lines with a ball point pen. Tack the braid along the lines, and secure very firmly but simply (pages *25* and *26* and diagram *3*). If preferred, the lines could be covered with bold feather stitch instead of using braid, but in either case, take care to keep the lines very straight.

Mark out and work a motif in each square, aiming at a good balance of colour, shape and detail. Cut a matching square of fabric for the back of the cushion, and join with a plain seam all round or an edging of covered piping cord.

Pentagon ball   colour plate *2* facing page *33*

This is an old but always popular idea with a new decorative look. Needlewomen have used it in many ways, but the basic plan remains the same, using twelve five-sided shapes. The ball is made from bright felt shapes, each embroidered with a different motif in black or white.

Two sizes for the pentagon shape are given in chart *10*. Decide which is required, cut a piece of iron-on *vilene* large enough approximately to take the shape twelve times. By laying the *vilene* on the chart, trace the shape twelve times. Cut out each one roughly a little larger all round, and with a warm iron press each, adhesive side down, to a different coloured piece of felt. Then cut out each section accurately. Mark out and embroider a different motif on each section.

The ball is made up in two halves, each having one section surrounded by five others. Join these with fine strong sewing on the right side (diagram *12a*). Then join the edges of the five sections to make a cup shape with serrated edges (diagram *12b*). Fit the two cups together and join all round. When only two sections remain open, fill the ball with foam crumbs or any soft filling, and com-

89

plete the seaming. If a rattle is needed, put a few beads into a tiny box, and insert it into the centre of the filling. Finally work along every edge with bold chain stitch, plain or whipped.

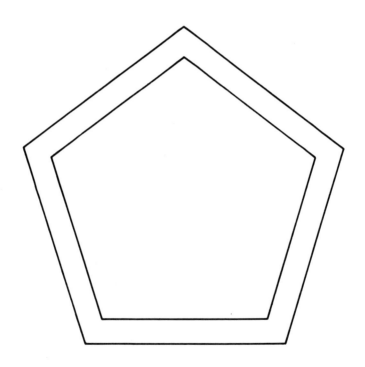

Chart 10   Pattern for pentagon ball in two sizes

a

b

Diagram 12   Two stages in making pentagon ball

Chart 11   Miscellaneous motifs

Chart 12   Miscellaneous motifs

Further reading

Patterns from Peasant Embroidery   Margaret Beautement   Batsford London   Branford Massachusetts

Cross Stitch Patterns   Thelma M Nye   Batsford London   Van Nostrand Reinhold New York

Embroidery for the Home   Jean Kinmond   Batsford London Branford Massachusetts

Simple Stitches   Anne Butler   Batsford London   Praeger New York

Anchor Manual of Needlework   J & P Coats   Batsford London Branford Massachusetts

Canvas Embroidery   Diana Springall   Batsford London   Branford Massachusetts

Ideas for Canvas Work   Mary Rhodes   Batsford London   Branford Massachusetts

Handbook of Stitches   Grete Petersen and Elsie Svennas   Batsford London   Van Nostrand Reinhold New York

Lettering for Embroidery   Pat Russell   Batsford London   Van Nostrand Reinhold New York

Inspiration for Embroidery   Constance Howard   Batsford London Branford Massachusetts

Design in Embroidery   Kathleen Whyte   Batsford London   Branford Massachusetts

Creative Stitches   Edith John   Batsford London   Branford Massachusetts

Filling Stitches   Edith John   Batsford London   Branford Massachusetts

Needleweaving   Edith John   Batsford London   Branford Massachusetts

Suppliers

Most of the items mentioned in this book can be obtained from any large department store or needlecraft shop, or from handicraft suppliers.

Some useful details are given below. For postal enquiries always state what is required and enclose a stamped addressed envelope.

Great Britain

Threads, fabrics and embroidery accessories

Harrods Limited   Brompton Road   London   SW1
John Lewis and Company Limited   Oxford Street   London   W1
Fred Aldous Limited   37 Lever Street   Manchester   M60 1UX
Mrs Mary Allen   Turnditch   Derbyshire
Art Needlework Industries Limited   7 St Michael's Mansions   Ship Street   Oxford
Mrs Patricia Coole   12 Kingsley Avenue   Banstead   Surrey
Dryad Limited   Northgate   Leicester
B Francis   4 Glentworth Street   London NW1
The Felt and Hessian Shop   34 Grenville Street   London EC1
Thomas Hunter Limited   36 Northumberland Street   Newcastle upon Tyne   NE1 7DS
I M Jervie   21-23 West Port   Arbroath   Angus   Scotland
The Ladies Work Society Limited   Delabere House   New Road   Moreton-in-Marsh   Gloucestershire   *London showroom*   138 Brompton Road   London   SW3
Mace and Nairn   89 Crane Street   Salisbury   Wiltshire
The Needlewoman Shop   146 Regent Street   London   W1
Nottingham Handicraft Company   Melton Road   West Bridgford   Nottingham
The Royal School of Needlework   25 Princes Gate   South Kensington   London   SW7
Mrs Joan Trickett   110 Marsden Road   Burnley   Lancashire
Betty Veal   Waterloo Buildings   Vernon Walk   London Road   Southampton   SO1 2AD
The Wool Shop and the Home Artistic Limited   89-90 Darlington Street   Wolverhampton

Vilene and felt are obtainable from many of the firms listed above
also from the majority of department stores

Iron-on embroidery transfers for the borders shown in this book are
obtainable only from Ruby Evans   2 Erroll Road   Romford
Essex   (UK only)

USA

Threads and embroidery accessories

Bucky King Embroideries Unlimited   121 South Drive   Pittsburgh
Pennsylvania   15238

American Crewel Studio   Box 553   Westfield   New Jersey
07091

American Thread Corporation   90 Park Avenue   New York   NY

Appleton Brothers of London   West Main Road   Little Compton
Rhode Island   02837

The Needle's Point Studio   1626 Macon Street   McLean   Virgina
22101

Yarn Depot   545 Sutter Street   San Francisco 94102